LOVING

MYSELF

NOTEBOOK

ISBN: 978-1-958191-00-2

THIS NOTEBOOK
BELONGS TO

_____

_____

Loving Myself Notebook is dedicated to YOU! It is a space for you to reflect, dream, be inspired, share your feelings, and become more conscious of the beauty and miracle that is you and your dreams in life. With magical scenery as the backdrop, the affirmations and brief exercises will guide you on a journey of self reflection and greater consciousness to transform your life to the happiness that you deserve.

You can simply use it as a journal without doing the brief exercises. However, if you choose to do the exercises, see them more as an opportunity for exploration and becoming more intimate with yourself rather than a chore.

May it be a guide to bring out your light from the shadows.

I am beautiful.
Write 3 positive qualities about yourself.

....
....
....
....
....
....
....
....
....
....
....
....
....
....
....
....
....
....
....
....
....
....
....
....
....

I am beautiful.

....
....
....
....
....
....
....
....
....
....
....
....
....
....
....
....
....
....
....
....
....
....
....
....
....
....
....
....

I see beauty all around me.
Write 3 beautiful things that you saw today.

I see beauty all around me.

I nourish my body.

Drink 6-8 glasses of warm, pure water today.

....
....
....
....
....
....
....
....
....
....
....
....
....
....
....
....
....
....
....
....
....
....
....
....
....

I nourish my body.

....
....
....
....
....
....
....
....
....
....
....
....
....
....
....
....
....
....
....
....
....
....
....
....
....

I bow down to the morning sun.

Meditate. Fill yourself with the rays of the sun.

....

....

....

....

....

....

....

....

....

....

....

....

....

....

....

....

....

....

....

....

....

....

....

....

I bow down to the morning sun.

I take time to listen to my heart.

What is your heart feeling?

....
....
....
....
....
....
....
....
....
....
....
....
....
....
....
....
....
....
....
....
....
....
....
....
....
....

I take time to listen to my heart.

....
....
....
....
....
....
....
....
....
....
....
....
....
....
....
....
....
....
....
....
....
....
....

I forgive those that have hurt me.

Write the names of those who have hurt you and send them prayers and good wishes.

....
....
....
....
....
....
....
....
....
....
....
....
....
....
....
....
....
....
....
....
....
....
....
....
....
....
....
....

I forgive those that have hurt me.

I am kind and gentle with myself.
Write 3 things that you love about yourself.

I am kind and gentle with myself.

I nourish my body with healthy food.
Eat 3 different vegetables and fruits today.

....
....
....
....
....
....
....
....
....
....
....
....
....
....
....
....
....
....
....
....
....
....
....
....
....
....
....

I nourish my body with healthy food.

··
··
··
··
··
··
··
··
··
··
··
··
··
··
··
··
··
··
··
··
··
··
··
··
··
··

My home is my temple.

Clean your home from top to bottom.

···
···
···
···
···
···
···
···
···
···
···
···
···
···
···
···
···
···
···
···
···
···
···
···
···

My home is my temple.

....
....
....
....
....
....
....
....
....
....
....
....
....
....
....
....
....
....
....
....
....
....
....
....
....

I simplify my life.
Clear the clutter from your bedroom.

....
....
....
....
....
....
....
....
....
....
....
....
....
....
....
....
....
....
....
....
....
....
....
....
....
....

I simplify my life.

....
....
....
....
....
....
....
....
....
....
....
....
....
....
....
....
....
....
....
....
....
....
....
....

I allow my body to rest.
Sleep at least 8 hours and let your body reset.

....
....
....
....
....
....
....
....
....
....
....
....
....
....
....
....
....
....
....
....
....
....
....
....
....
....
....
....
....

I allow my body to rest.

I bow down to the radiant moon.
Meditate. Fill yourself with the light of the moon.

....
....
....
....
....
....
....
....
....
....
....
....
....
....
....
....
....
....
....
....
....
....

I bow down to the radiant moon.

I forgive myself.
Write down 3 things you have regretted
and forgive yourself.

I forgive myself.

I pamper myself.

Do something healthy that gives you joy.

I pamper myself.

I nourish my mind.

Turn off all distractions and quiet your mind.

I nourish my mind.

I let go of all that doesn't serve me.

Detox your body by eating lots of fruits and
vegetables and drinking enough water.

....
....
....
....
....
....
....
....
....
....
....
....
....
....
....
....
....
....
....
....
....
....
....
....

I let go of all that doesn't serve me.

....
....
....
....
....
....
....
....
....
....
....
....
....
....
....
....
....
....
....
....
....
....
....
....
....

I release any anger I'm holding onto.

Write down 3 people you feel anger towards
and feel it dissolving.

....
....
....
....
....
....
....
....
....
....
....
....
....
....
....
....
....
....
....
....
....
....
....
....
....

I release any anger I'm holding onto.

I allow my light to shine.

Write down your special gifts.

I allow my light to shine.

My words are a tool for blessing.

Say something kind to 3 people.

My words are a tool for blessing.

....
....
....
....
....
....
....
....
....
....
....
....
....
....
....
....
....
....
....
....
....
....
....

I love my body.
Spend some time exercising and feeling alive.

I love my body.

....
....
....
....
....
....
....
....
....
....
....
....
....
....
....
....
....
....
....
....
....
....
....
....
....

I feel light.

Clear the clutter in your living room.

I feel light.

I feel good about myself.

Enjoy a deep, relaxing massage.

··

··

··

··

··

··

··

··

··

··

··

··

··

··

··

··

··

··

··

··

··

··

··

··

··

··

··

I feel good about myself.

....
....
....
....
....
....
....
....
....
....
....
....
....
....
....
....
....
....
....
....
....
....
....
....
....
....

I feel happy.

Write down 3 happy memories from your childhood.

....
....
....
....
....
....
....
....
....
....
....
....
....
....
....
....
....
....
....
....
....
....
....
....
....
....
....
....

I feel happy.

....
....
....
....
....
....
....
....
....
....
....
....
....
....
....
....
....
....
....
....
....
....
....
....
....
....
....

I am confident.

Breathe deeply for 2 minutes.

I am confident.

....
....
....
....
....
....
....
....
....
....
....
....
....
....
....
....
....
....
....
....
....
....
....
....
....
....
....
....

I am healthy.

Avoid refined sugar and junk food.

I am healthy.

....
....
....
....
....
....
....
....
....
....
....
....
....
....
....
....
....
....
....
....
....
....
....
....
....

I am peaceful.

Play soothing music and quiet your mind.

I am peaceful.

I am worthy of joy.

Try something you have never tried before.

....
....
....
....
....
....
....
....
....
....
....
....
....
....
....
....
....
....
....
....
....
....
....
....
....
....
....
....
....

I am worthy of joy.

I love myself.

Do something nice for yourself today.

I love myself.

I feel alive.

Visualize a golden light in the center of your chest
filling up your entire body.

....
....
....
....
....
....
....
....
....
....
....
....
....
....
....
....
....
....
....
....
....
....
....
....
....
....
....
....
....
....

I feel alive.

I attract positive people in my life.
Write the name of 3 people that uplift you.

....

....

....

....

....

....

....

....

....

....

....

....

....

....

....

....

....

....

....

....

....

....

....

....

....

I attract positive people in my life.

....
....
....
....
....
....
....
....
....
....
....
....
....
....
....
....
....
....
....
....
....
....
....
....
....

I am love.

Give a gift to someone - even if it's just a smile.

....
....
....
....
....
....
....
....
....
....
....
....
....
....
....
....
....
....
....
....
....
....
....
....
....
....

I am love.

....
....
....
....
....
....
....
....
....
....
....
....
....
....
....
....
....
....
....
....
....
....
....
....

I am surrounded by people who love me.

Write the name of 3 people that make you feel loved.

I am surrounded by people who love me.

....
....
....
....
....
....
....
....
....
....
....
....
....
....
....
....
....
....
....
....
....
....
....
....
....

I live consciously.
Meditate. Sit under a tree and feel your oneness.

I live consciously.

....
....
....
....
....
....
....
....
....
....
....
....
....
....
....
....
....
....
....
....
....
....
....
....
....
....
....
....

I feel free.

Write 3 things that you always wanted to do and
make a plan to do them.

....
....
....
....
....
....
....
....
....
....
....
....
....
....
....
....
....
....
....
....
....
....
....
....
....
....
....

I feel free.

··
··
··
··
··
··
··
··
··
··
··
··
··
··
··
··
··
··
··
··
··
··
··
··
··

I am aligned.

Meditate. Feel the stars showering you with
inspiration on your path.

....
....
....
....
....
....
....
....
....
....
....
....
....
....
....
....
....
....
....
....
....
....
....
....
....
....
....

I am aligned.

I am fearless.

Write down 3 places you always wanted to
visit and begin planning it.

I am fearless.

....
....
....
....
....
....
....
....
....
....
....
....
....
....
....
....
....
....
....
....
....
....
....
....
....

I embrace my uniqueness.
Write 3 things that are unique about you.

···
···
···
···
···
···
···
···
···
···
···
···
···
···
···
···
···
···
···
···
···
···
···
···
···

I embrace my uniqueness.

....
....
....
....
....
....
....
....
....
....
....
....
....
....
....
....
....
....
....
....
....
....
....
....
....

I take good care of myself.

Write 3 things you have neglected to do for
yourself and make a point of doing them.

I take good care of myself.

....
....
....
....
....
....
....
....
....
....
....
....
....
....
....
....
....
....
....
....
....
....
....
....
....

I am strong.

Meditate. Feel yourself one with a mountain and embodying it's strength.

I am strong.

....
....
....
....
....
....
....
....
....
....
....
....
....
....
....
....
....
....
....
....
....
....
....
....
....

I am vibrant.

Write down 3 steps you can take towards
being healthier.

....
....
....
....
....
....
....
....
....
....
....
....
....
....
....
....
....
....
....
....
....
....
....
....
....
....

I am vibrant.

My life is a gift.

Write 3 things that life has blessed you with.

My life is a gift.

I give thanks to all my ancestors.
Offer prayers to all your ancestors.

I give thanks to all my ancestors.

....
....
....
....
....
....
....
....
....
....
....
....
....
....
....
....
....
....
....
....
....
....
....
....
....
....
....

I am amazing.

See yourself through the eyes of divinity.

....
....
....
....
....
....
....
....
....
....
....
....
....
....
....
....
....
....
....
....
....
....
....

I am amazing.

....
....
....
....
....
....
....
....
....
....
....
....
....
....
....
....
....
....
....
....
....
....
....
....
....

I believe in myself.

Visualize yourself looking and radiating exactly how
you wish yourself to be.

....
....
....
....
....
....
....
....
....
....
....
....
....
....
....
....
....
....
....
....
....
....
....
....
....
....
....
....
....

I believe in myself.

I take responsibility for my life.
Write 3 things that you have been procrastinating
and make a point to do them by a certain date.

I take responsibility for my life.

I am abundant.

Visualize your life exactly how you wish it to be.

I am abundant.

....
....
....
....
....
....
....
....
....
....
....
....
....
....
....
....
....
....
....
....
....
....
....
....

I am a miracle.
Make 3 wishes.

....
....
....
....
....
....
....
....
....
....
....
....
....
....
....
....
....
....
....
....
....
....
....
....
....

I am a miracle.

....
....
....
....
....
....
....
....
....
....
....
....
....
....
....
....
....
....
....
....
....
....
....
....
....
....
....
....
....

I enjoy my own company.

Spend a whole day all by yourself.

I enjoy my own company.

I am true to myself.

Take time to listen to your inner wisdom and follow it.

I am true to myself.

....
....
....
....
....
....
....
....
....
....
....
....
....
....
....
....
....
....
....
....
....
....
....
....
....
....
....
....

I let go of guilt.

Write 3 things you feel guilty about and forgive yourself.

I let go of guilt.

I allow myself to heal.

Take time for a retreat and allow yourself to realign.

....
....
....
....
....
....
....
....
....
....
....
....
....
....
....
....
....
....
....
....
....
....
....
....
....
....
....
....

I allow myself to heal.

I listen to my soul.

Meditate. Sit quietly and open yourself to listening to
what your soul is trying to share with you.

I listen to my soul.

I trust myself.

Repeat this affirmation to yourself frequently.

I trust myself.

I feel safe.
Write 3 situations that make you feel safe and 3 that do not.

....
....
....
....
....
....
....
....
....
....
....
....
....
....
....
....
....
....
....
....
....
....
....
....
....
....
....
....

I feel safe.

I am open to receive love.

Meditate. See yourself as a flower - gentle and innocent.

I am open to receive love.

I am blossoming.

Visualize yourself full of life and happy.

....
....
....
....
....
....
....
....
....
....
....
....
....
....
....
....
....
....
....
....
....
....
....
....
....
....
....

I am blossoming.

I free myself from fear.
Write down 1 thing that you are afraid of.
Pray to become free of this fear.

I free myself from fear.

....
....
....
....
....
....
....
....
....
....
....
....
....
....
....
....
....
....
....
....
....
....
....
....
....
....
....

I observe my emotions with love.

Emotions are like the weather, ever changing. Be present with your most dominant emotion and feel it without reacting or judging.

....

....

....

....

....

....

....

....

....

....

....

....

....

....

....

....

....

....

....

....

....

....

....

....

....

....

....

....

....

....

I observe my emotions with love.

I am honest with myself.

Write 3 wonderful qualities about yourself and 3 that
are harder to admit.

I am honest with myself.

I see goodness all around me.

Write 3 situations which you believe are unpleasant
and see the potential goodness in them.

I see goodness all around me.

I choose wisely.

Write a situation that you are indecisive about.
In 2 columns write all the potential positive and negative
about it.

....
....
....
....
....
....
....
....
....
....
....
....
....
....
....
....
....
....
....
....
....
....
....
....
....

I choose wisely.

I take time for myself.

Put aside 30 minutes every day only for yourself.

....
....
....
....
....
....
....
....
....
....
....
....
....
....
....
....
....
....
....
....
....
....
....
....
....

I take time for myself.

....
....
....
....
....
....
....
....
....
....
....
....
....
....
....
....
....
....
....
....
....
....
....
....
....
....
....
....
....

I am open to wonderful possibilities.

Feel the joy of great opportunities coming into your life.

....
....
....
....
....
....
....
....
....
....
....
....
....
....
....
....
....
....
....
....
....
....
....
....
....
....
....
....
....

I am open to wonderful possibilities.

I am humble.

True empowerment comes with humility.

I am humble.

··

··

··

··

··

··

··

··

··

··

··

··

··

··

··

··

··

··

··

··

··

··

··

··

··

··

··

··

I am whole.

Visualize many pieces of a puzzle all coming together and forming your body.

I am whole.

Today will be a perfect day.

Breathe in happiness. Breathe out sadness.

Today will be a perfect day.

....
....
....
....
....
....
....
....
....
....
....
....
....
....
....
....
....
....
....
....
....
....
....
....
....
....

My life is filled with grace.

Write 3 affirmations for yourself and repeat them daily.

....
....
....
....
....
....
....
....
....
....
....
....
....
....
....
....
....
....
....
....
....
....
....
....
....
....
....

My life is filled with grace.

....
....
....
....
....
....
....
....
....
....
....
....
....
....
....
....
....
....
....
....
....
....
....
....

I respect myself.

Look at yourself in the mirror and say 'I respect myself.

I respect myself.

I have faith.

Trust that you are guided and protected on your path.

I have faith.

I vow to love myself fully.

May you be blessed in every step that you take and may
your life be filled with joy, peace, love, good health
and abundance.

....

....

....

....

....

....

....

....

....

....

....

....

....

....

....

....

....

....

....

....

....

....

....

....

....

....

....

....

....

I vow to love myself fully.

I vow to love myself fully.

....
....
....
....
....
....
....
....
....
....
....
....
....
....
....
....
....
....
....
....
....
....
....
....
....
....
....

I vow to love myself fully.

OTHER BOOKS
by Rita Panahi

- "Own Your Health Change Your Destiny"
- "Lose Weight Unleash Your Creativity"
- "How to Change Your Karma Now"
- "Simple Relationship Wisdom"

Stay Connected:

- www.facebook.com/RitaPanahiAuthor
- www.facebook.com/groups/RitaPanahiAuthor
- www.instagram.com/RitaPanahiAuthor
- web: www.RitaPanahi.com
- web: www.Author.RitaPanahi.com

ABOUT THE AUTHOR

Rita Panahi, L.Ac., Dipl.O.M. holds a master's in Chinese medicine, a five thousand-year-old medicine. She is an author of 4 books and an award winning filmmaker of the documentary 'Ayni'. Having trained with indigenous healers for over 25 years, she combines her artistic creativity and her depth in knowledge for human transformation into *Loving Myself Notebook* to bring the opportunity for others to be happy and make their dreams into a reality.

www.ingramcontent.com/pod-product-compliance
Lightning Source LLC
Chambersburg PA
CBHW071153120626
46546CB00006B/2249